Anthony Burgess

by Carol M. Dix

No. 2

Anthony Burgess is one of the very few authors who combine a high standard of writing with a high rate of output—he has published eighteen novels between the years 1956 and 1971. In his fiction he has paid special attention to the conflicts and discords to which contemporary society is liable during a period of rapid transition. Some of these developments Burgess has observed at first hand: much of his material relates to his experience as a teacher in the Colonial Service and as an expatriate with idealized memories of England who returns to find it 'a society anæsthetized by television, supermarkets, pop singers and strikes'. Burgess's upbringing as a Catholic, with its emphasis on traditional values, has done much, Miss Dix considers, to mould his philosophical approach and accounts for his witty castigation of what he regards as meretricious in contemporary standards. Commenting on his style, especially in such novels as *A Clockwork Orange*, *Nothing like the Sun*, and *MF*, she remarks that his feeling for words is more aural than visual. His mode of writing has been strongly influenced by his exceptional gifts as a musician and as a linguist. He is an author who takes an evident delight in the manipulation of the English language and, like James Joyce, of whom he is a devoted admirer, he often uses words which he has invented himself.

Miss Dix obtained an Honours degree in English and American literature at the University of Manchester and subsequently joined *The Guardian*. She is now on the staff of the Features Department of *The Guardian*'s London office and is a frequent contributor to the paper.

20p net

ANTHONY BURGESS

ANTHONY BURGESS

by

CAROL M. DIX

Edited by Ian Scott-Kilvert

PUBLISHED FOR
THE BRITISH COUNCIL
BY LONGMAN GROUP LTD

LONGMAN GROUP LTD
Longman House, Burnt Mill, Harlow, Essex

*Associated companies, branches and
representatives throughout the world*

First published 1971

© Carol M. Dix, 1971

*Printed in Great Britain by
F. Mildner & Sons, London, EC1R 5EJ*

SBN 0 582 01218 X

ANTHONY BURGESS

I. THE LIFE

JOHN Anthony Burgess Wilson drops the ends of his name, or rather as he describes it, pulls the cracker of his name to reveal the pseudonym; a name to him is like a toy or paper hat. Reading the wealth of his novels, criticism, essays, reviews, and journalism one can similarly peel off layer upon layer of his life. He hides nothing. His own experience is the touchstone or the setting for novels that comment on contemporary life, on racial harmonies in our colonies, on modern suburban England, on human nature and the cyclic patterns of history, on the role of the artist and his relationship with society, even on the very nature of artistic inspiration, whom and why it attacks.

He began writing novels seriously in his early forties after service in the army and a career as a teacher both in England and abroad with the colonial civil service. It is almost as if everything before then in his life had been an accumulation of experience and material for his novels. Autobiographical facts leap from the pages. Born in 1917, in Manchester, the son of a pianist father and music-hall mother, beautiful Belle Burgess who died when he was a baby, he was brought up under the influence of a stepmother who reappears as the grotesque figure in *Inside Mr Enderby*. The other dominant influence in his life both at home and at school has been the Roman Catholic Church, which is described in many of his novels. In the early chapters of *Tremor of Intent*, for example, he uses his childhood memories of the Xaverian College, Manchester, to paint a delightful portrait of growing schoolboys' minds as they face the deadening impenetrability of Catholic doctrines. Burgess has a remarkable ability and facility with languages of all kinds and with words in general. He wrote poetry as a boy (F. X. Enderby's poetry is, of course, his own), but he originally intended to be a musician. A failed physics matriculation exam kept him out of the music course at Manchester University, so he

3

studied English language and literature and has been
fascinated by the close relationship between words and
music, in a Joycean way, ever since.

His first novel (written in 1949) concerned the life of a
failed musician. Richard Ennis in *A Vision of Battlements*
is the first of Burgess's anti-heroes who is in the cruel
process of learning about his failures, and not only in music
either. For the novel is significantly set in Gibraltar, in the
post-war period when the soldiers are waiting around to
be given something to do. The setting is real. Burgess
wanted to write about the conflict of feelings, of lives and
ideas he experienced in Gibraltar; about the experience of
leaving England, its moderate climate and tepid passions;
about arriving in Continental lands where there may be
more sin, more violence, and more evil, but to him, a
Catholic, that was the only real way of life. The novel was
not published for many years (1965), because it still pained
him. In between he wrote and published the Malayan
trilogy, inspired by his teaching in Malaya and Borneo
where he found, in the conflict of races and the tensions
between the colonizing British and the independent-minded
Malays, the 'confluence of cultures', the subject matter of
many novels.

But Burgess's vision of the anti-hero is barbed with
humour. He writes in a style of comic satire, similar to
Evelyn Waugh, that again can be seen to derive from his
personal experience of life. In 1959, he was invalided home
from Malaya and his work with the colonial civil service,
with a suspected brain tumour. Given a year to live, this
man's remarkable resourcefulness led him to write five
novels in that year, so as to leave his wife some posthumous
income. He wrote *The Doctor is Sick*, drawing on his own
near tragic situation; also *Inside Enderby*, *The Worm and the
Ring*, *The Wanting Seed*, and *One Hand Clapping*: for the
first and the last of these novels he used another pseudonym,
Joseph Kell, as publishers and critics frowned on such
productivity.

Since then he has written eight more novels, seven critical books and one biographical book on Shakespeare. He has written at least two television plays, five or six screenplays, a mountain of book reviews and articles for both English and American journals. He has visited Leningrad for material for his novels, been widowed and remarried in the same year to an Italian *contessa*, emigrated to Malta with much press coverage of his angry statements about the tax laws in England on writers' incomes, and now lives either in Malta, Italy or in America, where he stays as a resident writer in American universities. Two of his novels, *A Clockwork Orange* and *The Wanting Seed* have become popular among American students, in the same way as Tolkien's or Huxley's for their magical other-worldliness.

It seems to be a life story of its own overwhelming proportions, yet Anthony Burgess claims that he lives a very quiet life, preferring to read or listen to (or play) music rather than to suffer the society of other people. The facts are there in his writings; his essays collected in *Urgent Copy* (1968) reveal even more of his life's story. He does not write out of any great didactic vocation to preach, to teach or to surmise. His novels are funny; they are witty, imaginative, very clever, informed and above all entertaining. We learn certain things of the man—that he is an intensely active thinker whose philosophies stem from an Augustinian Catholic upbringing; that his approach to writing is through the sound of the word and that he loves to play linguistic games, enjoys punning and theorizing on the meaning of words and language and that the only writers he envies or emulates are Shakespeare, James Joyce and Vladimir Nabokov. He sees himself, the artist, as an objective animal, withdrawn and contemplative, uninvolved and uncommitted. He sees humanity as doomed to some ironic comedy. Its aims, its loves, its ideals, are pathetic. He prefers to live in the past, in exile, or in a rarefied world of literature and music. His writing cannot really be categorized, but for convenience I have split my discussion of the novels into three sections: the first deals with novels of social realism and satire; the second with the more philosophical novels, and the last with the novels which display his interest in language and the art of creation from words.

II. THE COMEDY

Burgess is a contemporary of such English writers as Kingsley Amis and Angus Wilson, and he shares with them in his early novels certain traits such as a decided traditionalism and a preference for provincial or local subject matter. It has been said of today's English writers that they are too concerned with England's past. Burgess, however, brings new light to old themes, writing as an exile, with an objective eye cast both on the colonies and on England. Much good literary work is concerned with watersheds in time, the changes of values involved in some process of history. In his earlier novels, Burgess sees both the colonies *Time for a Tiger* (1956), *The Enemy in the Blanket* (1958), *Beds in the East* (1959) (Malayan Trilogy), *Devil of a State* (1961), and *A Vision of Battlements* (1965), and also England *The Right to an Answer* (1960), and *The Worm and the Ring* (1961), as passing through phases of transition.

His views of both types of environment share that wry tone, which when dramatized becomes comic irony. In Malaya, for example, he sees a melting-pot of races: Malays, Chinese, Tamils, Sikhs, Eurasians and British, and sees them all as openly contemptuous of the other. Here is no liberal humanism of the school of Angus Wilson: Burgess is a social realist, or perhaps pessimist, and he drops no hints of a better, more united future. Yet he believes in imperialism, seeing the conflicts it creates as good for society (or for novelists at least). His view of England is of a contemporary society anaesthetized by the television, by supermarkets, pop singers and strikes. The conflict is there, too, though, in his love for the England of the past and his alienation from its present.

In an essay in *Urgent Copy*, writing about his introduction to the novelist's trade in Gibraltar, Burgess expressed surprise that his novels turned out to be comic. He sees himself as a man of gloom and sobriety. And his comedy has to be seen in this light. Not through the eyes of a man taking a gentle laugh at the world; it is rather the humour of one who finds a profound lack of things to believe in, who consequently finds little that is real to him and so he makes comedy. His comedy is keyed in the pessimistic tone of Shakespeare's 'As flies to wanton boys are we to the gods, they kill us for their sport', or the profound Augustinian despair of Graham Greene's *The Comedians*.

But Burgess's underlying despair is effectively offset by the vividness of the characters with whom he sports. The central character of The Malayan Trilogy (in American publications called *The Long Day Wanes*) is Victor Crabbe, a man who has come to teach in Malaya out of a fervent belief, at first, that this is what he was meant to do. No other colonialist, however, allows him to rest for long in this belief. The cynics soon make it clear that he came because there was no other job for him at the time. The Malays and the Chinese also make it clear that they don't want him. They want independence. The novels pinpoint the lazy, decadent, but essentially kind and liberal English characters, and the very different Malays and Tamils, with the delightful and colourful Alladad Khan (who courteously woos Crabbe's wife, Fenella) and the homosexual Ibrahim. It contrasts ancient Asian traditions in the Moslem world with the crumbling British traditions.

The Crabbes's marriage, for instance, is shown in two stages. In *Time for a Tiger*, Fenella is horrified by Victor's affair with the Malay girl Rahimah; by *The Enemy in the Blanket*, Victor is flirting dangerously, in such a narrow community, with Ann, another British exile's wife, and Fenella realizes that it is up to her to leave him. Crabbe is suffering from a lost first wife whom he can never stop loving. He feels fond of Fenella, but guilty of what he is not capable of giving her. He hesitates and is indecisive. The conflicts in their marriage are set against a background of terrible heat, and forest skirmishes as the Communists try to take over the Malaysian province. Some of the best scenes weld all these elements; such as the trip with Alladad Khan and Nabby Adams to the north of the country to see an encampment of primitive people. Nabby Adams is a wonderful picture of decadent Britishdom, a warm-hearted, gregarious alcoholic who leans on the crumbling Crabbes for his only security.

Their little trip is doomed. They end up being ambushed in a skirmish. And as usual nothing is resolved. The delay brings another theme in the story to a head. Victor has constant trouble at the school, where his white imperialist presence is not wanted. At the previous school they discovered a Communist past; now again they are busy accusing him of Communist infiltration and influence on the boys. The day he is late is the day of the school sports. The boys have ganged up together, as schoolboys will, with Communist help (but not Crabbe's) and bring the sports day to a silent halt. No one will take part in any event. The school sports day is a perfect example of English manners transposed straight and unmodified into a different society, and the scene a brilliant illustration of the farcical elements of these societies clashing and not mixing.

The Worm and the Ring and *The Right to an Answer* are both about Burgess's feelings towards England. Once more they offer objective portraits of a country in transition, but the views are more personally slanted, for they involve Burgess's own Catholic background and his contempt for a civilization of suburban streets, television aerials and lack of moral and ethical standards; whether it be the low pay and status awarded to teachers, 'indigent as medieval clerks', or the suburban wife-swapping in a Midlands town. Denham is surprised to find that this practice causes chaos, for, as he says, 'I thought the idea was to swap partners at weekends. An innocent suburban game like tennis.'

The Worm and the Ring is the more sympathetic novel, though it wanders too much in the gloom of despair. Howarth is the epitome of Burgess's sometimes self-indulgent intellectual despair. A grammar school teacher, he reads Rilke, 'Who, if he were to cry would hear him among the angelic order?' and can feel only pity, not love, for his son Peter, who will have to go through the same life. His wife Veronica, his son Peter, and himself share no joy, no generosity or enthusiasm for life. Their humdrum existence is Burgess's view of English life which offers un-rewarding teaching, followed by halves of cider in the local pub. Similar feelings are expressed in *The Right to an Answer*, more cuttingly through Denham the narrator, who des-cribes Sunday visits to his sister's house for lunch, travelling by bus, as a '. . . gape of Sunday ennui. So we Sundayed along, rattling, and creaking in Sunday hollowness.'

Christopher Howarth begins to be involved in life when he meets Hilda Connor, another teacher. She reawakens his sexuality and introduces some vitality into his life. The novel is firmly based on Burgess's own teaching experience whilst in England, at a grammar school in Banbury. Un-fortunately, one of his characters was too lifelike, and although the book was originally published in 1961, few copies were available until revisions were made and it was reissued in 1970.

The narrative involves a secret diary kept by one of the schoolgirls which is exploited by an up-and-coming young teacher, Gardiner, in his play for the headship of, one day, the whole complex of local comprehensive schools. Burgess sees Gardiner as a specimen of the new breed of Englishmen. Whilst this new England is growing out of the old, he sees no place for those still living in the past. The end of the novel trails off rather weakly with Howarth suddenly achieving both the money and the sense of direction to emigrate to Italy.

They were going to seek the other half of themselves in an exile which was not wholly exile, for England had not been completely a home for them and their kind for nearly four centuries.

Fortunately Burgess does not oversimplify to the extent of wrapping Veronica and Peter neatly up in this parcel. They are allowed their regrets, but also feel that to be in England is to compromise.

In *The Right to an Answer*, the narrator, Denham, gives the novel a similarly weak ending by executing a sudden volte-face and changing the views he has stood by so strongly throughout the novel. The novel's great strength is the exile's loveless, objective view of England. The novel carries Burgess's form of social humour to its furthest extent, creating what today would be called 'black comedy', as the social satire goes on to include murder upon murder.

Denham is a voluntary exile home on a brief leave (as was Burgess). He stays with his father in a small Midlands industrial town, where he becomes involved with the small-minded community, entangled in their attempts at adultery and escape, and is horrified by their insensitive destruction of what he sees as the principal asset of their life, stability. But the Midlands town also becomes inadvertently involved in another form of destruction, through Mr Raj, a friendly, garrulous, Singhalese sociologist who at first seems only too willing to be accepted into the community, for what, we later find, are insidious reasons.

Raj and his ancestors have been ruled by the paternalistic British for so long that he wants to gain some revenge, and the way to do this is to become the father himself. He kills old Mr Denham by suffocating him paternalistically (and farcically), with curry. The blackness of the comedy only really becomes apparent as Raj starts to shoot his beloved Alice's wayward husband, and then himself; the two dying together on the bed beneath a painting of *The Last Watch of Hero*. Denham's contempt and sympathy for their pathetic lives is vividly dramatized in this tale of a feeble suburban passion, which is diluted even further by television.

The police laugh at the report of such murders. Go home
and watch television they say. Burgess laughs too at 'Hero-
Alice', who is waiting for 'her weekly lover Leander-Jack
Brownlow, perhaps to swim the stormy straits for a night
of Pimms No. 1 and love'.

But in spite of his attacks upon England, some of his
strongest writing, his most characteristically witty and
imaginative language is used in these two novels, where
words are used for the aural as much as the visual image
and for the literary connotations. The best writing is found
perhaps in the descriptions of the England he loves to
remember. In *The Worm and the Ring*, he describes a small
English town on its market day in language reminiscent of
either a Shakespeare, Hopkins, or a Dylan Thomas:

> A bleating sale of grazing legs, ewes and couples was on. The town
> was rich today in the blessed beasthood of the older gods, brown and
> red and golden through the drizzle.

These browns and reds and golds are symbolic of a life
more vibrant, more exotic, more sinful, more primitive,
even, than Burgess finds in contemporary England. This is
an important theme in his writing, the search for the past,
almost for a Golden Age. It is something he found (or so
he tells us in the last essay of *Urgent Copy* (1968)), on
arriving as a soldier in Gibraltar, where he felt inspired by
the European environment to write. Brought up as a
Catholic, he identifies with that type of society and has
said that if it had not been for the Reformation, England
would have been a better place and not the country of
television, the Beatles and strikes that it seems to him.

What he perceives in England is an Eliot-like 'spiritual
death', such as is evoked in *The Waste Land*, with Prufrock-
like characters wandering around in an atmosphere of
hesitation and inertia. This theme is skilfully embodied in
the figures of withdrawn, passive or despairing characters,
often his anti-heroes, that people most of his books. It is
important to notice the different methods which he uses
to portray them; for he uses intellectual, sexual and creative

sterility to embody this theme. Victor Crabbe, in the Malayan trilogy, for example, is the impassive or, more subtly, the impotent central character, unable to give anything to Fenella. Similar anti-heroes are Denham, Christopher Howarth and Richard Ennis (*A Vision of Battlements*). Denham is left deliberately cool and uninvolved to narrate the events and pass objective comments. Howarth, Crabbe and Ennis, however, are asexual and their lives sterile.

Burgess develops this character in Edwin Spindrift in *The Doctor is Sick* (1960). Spindrift, a linguist, is a man more at home with words than life, who really cannot cope with a world 'where words are attached to things'; and F. X. Enderby of the diptych *Inside Mr Enderby* and *Enderby Outside* is a similar creation, though here the image takes us into a cognate theme concerning energy and the nature of creativity, which is discussed in the last section of this pamphlet. Enderby is a poet, but his lack of involvement leaves him a minor poet, itself a symbol of sterility. His asexuality becomes the centre of many comic scenes, and Burgess puts it to his usual clever and imaginative uses. For Enderby indulges in Portnoy-like masturbation (see Philip Roth's *Portnoy's Complaint*) and even leaves a female predator in 'mid-orgasm' as he rushes to attend to the whims of his Muse.

This theme of inertia has been treated by many contemporary authors, but I will refer especially to the American writer John Barth, who in his character, Jacob Horner, in *The End of the Road*, describes the sensation as one inspired by Laöcoon. The legend is that Laöcoon through his inertia failed to prevent his sons from being killed. In an early critical work *English Literature: A Survey for Students* (1958), Burgess widens its associations with a reference to Robert Burton's *Anatomy of Melancholy*, a sixteenth-century work, which he sees as a treatise on the mental ailment from which Hamlet suffers; he describes this as 'an inability to make up one's mind, to perform necessary actions, or to get any pleasure out of life'.

This 'spiritual death' is seen as symptomatic of contemporary English society. In these novels, discussed in this section, Burgess is exploring his attitude to the concept of stability, by drawing a picture of contemporary life against a vision of the past. With reference to his novels of colonial life, he describes the conflict as a 'confluence of cultures'; the same holds true of his novels of English life, only the cultures are of the past and the present. Bernard Bergonzi in *The Situation of the Novel* (1970), describes this as a trend among contemporary English writers, to wander between nostalgia and nightmare. The nightmare is what Burgess wants to portray. Later he develops more sophisticated methods.

III. THE PHILOSOPHY

In *The Reaction of Experimentation in the English Novel, 1950-60* (1967), Rubin Rabinowitz makes a similar criticism to that expressed by Bergonzi, to the effect that English novelists are too content to live in the past, although he does admit that Anthony Burgess has, in *A Clockwork Orange* (1962), tried some successful experimentation. Rabinowitz fails to discuss the novel and indeed it has received surprisingly little attention from critics either in England or America. This oversight may well become more noticeable in the near future, as it seems likely that *A Clockwork Orange*, together with its counterpart *The Wanting Seed*, will be recognized as two of the more important *avant-garde* creations of the sixties. (Stanley Kubrick, who produced the mystical film *2001*, is now working on a film of *A Clockwork Orange*.)

A Clockwork Orange may not have been written in the year of the big five novels, but it was published only a year later. Yet it is the kind of book which one might well expect to hear required a lifetime of work from its author—not just another novel quickly written, to be followed by another in the same year. For Burgess's imaginative scope here not only encompasses a whole vision of society in the future, but is even stretched to the formation of a language, or vernacular, and neatly gives that society an identity, a history and a reality. The language experiment called 'nadsat' is the derivative vernacular of Alex and his gang of 'droogs', which is derived in turn from Burgess's own interest in linguistics and the history of language—see his work published a couple of years later, *Language Made Plain* (1964). The vernacular is cleverly based on odd bits of rhyming slang, it includes a little gypsy talk and its basic roots are Russian. It is not impossible to read, taking only a few pages before context and meaning make the language perfectly comprehensible. 'We gave this devotchka a tolchock on the litso and the krovvy came out of her mouth', which roughly translated means, we gave this girl a blow on the face and blood came out of her mouth.

Nothing is told about the history or whereabouts of this strange futuristic society, but the deductions are there in the language. The society obviously has been subject to both American and Russian intervention if not invasion. The derivative language, spoken by the young, probably indicates the effects of propaganda through subliminal penetration. This is not a difficult situation to imagine, and one not too far removed from our present. For those who are familiar with the history of languages, it is known that our own language today bears the traces of numerous invasions and the resulting influences on our people, most notably those of the Scandinavians, the Romans and the Normans. Alex and his gang are simply the products of an England which Burgess showed us in *The Right to an Answer*, pushed to its logical extreme. There he feared for England's sanity (under America's influence). The bourgeois middle class in the novel have become so quiet and so passive, that the young who have succeeded them have chosen evil as their way of life, as an assertion of the will.

They beat up old men, rape girls, and kill, with no qualms. They are cheerful and spirited in their criminality and Alex, despite his violence, will not listen to pop, but only to classical music. For the violence is not bad. It may be evil, but in terms of humanity it is better than inertia. Burgess's romantic view of violence in this light, is that of an old-fashioned traditionalist who can see no good in our levelled out, contemporary society, which leads to grey totalitarianism. These romantic views again stem from his Catholic upbringing of a strict, black Jansenist kind. He calls himself a sort of Catholic Jacobite, who hates our present-day pragmatic socialism, because as he explains in *Urgent Copy*, '. . . any political ideology that rejects original sin and believes in moral progress ought strictly to be viewed with suspicion by Catholics'.

It is this suspicion of our contemporary liberal humanism, of our willingness to reform rather than punish, to educate rather than discipline that is seen in *A Clockwork Orange*, as a traditionalist's fear of the future. Alex is eventually caught, in the novel, by the police and is punished for his crimes, by being sentenced to be 'cured'. He is given electric shock treatment and is told 'You have no power of choice any longer. You are committed to socially acceptable acts, a little machine capable only of doing good.' Obviously Burgess's feeling is that there is potentially more good in a man who deliberately chooses evil, than in one who is forced to be good. Men are what they are, and are not forced into being so by any social conditioning or pressures. Alex ends up as a free individual with all his criminal impulses and, incidentally, his love of music, returned. He is considerably matured and ends optimistically saying:

'Tomorrow is all like sweet flowers and turning vonny earth and the stars and the old luna up there and your old droog Alex all on his oddy knocky seeking like a mate.'

But then Alex has never been unlikeable. Even at his most violent he is charming, and witty as narrator-hero, comparable perhaps to *King Lear*'s Edmund, who has all the forces of nature and the audience on his side. Alex symbolizes violence as an act of assertion, as a positive force.

Burgess's fear, then, is passivity. In its human form it leads to the dulling of the spirit as happened to Denham, Crabbe, Ennis or Howarth. But the 'spiritual death' can also be seen in the wider context of a political or philosophical sterility which afflicts whole countries given over to a totalitarian view of life. Later—if we can use the critic's licence and jump now to a work published in 1966— Burgess wrote *Tremor of Intent* with a similar theme to *A Clockwork Orange*, which may not succeed like the latter as a novel, yet as a vehicle for expressing Burgess's philosophical theories it is an important work. If after examining *Tremor of Intent*, we return to *The Wanting Seed*, again set in the future and also published in 1962, this section will have dealt with the novels that are as much metaphysical discussions as novels of wit, and satire.

In his journalism, Burgess has made it clear that he was not impressed by what he calls Wilsonian pragmatism ('Letter from England', *Hudson Review*, Autumn 1966), which is his reference to Harold Wilson's form of socialism in the Labour government of England 1964-70. He hates the State and any way of life that is so dominated. One would not expect him, therefore, to be a great adherent to Communist principles. In 1961, Burgess visited Leningrad to gather material for a novel *Honey for the Bears* (1963), from which he invented a story of imagination, adventure and social satire on the mixed-up values and hostilities between East and West, commenting on the eagerness with which the Bears (Russians) lap up the Honey (American materialism). It is a novel of Burgess's usual strange adventures, witty dialogue and critical commentary on people's lives, but one that remains of minor stature. Yet that same material was to provide food for a far more adventurous novel, in which he tries to embody his quasitheological concept of the world in the form of a contemporary spy novel, *Tremor of Intent* (1966).

Burgess uses the cold war between the East and the West, and the spying game, a very contemporary *modus vivendi* that plants the book firmly in the present, as a metaphor for a life of indeterminate acts. What he wants life to be is a reflection of ultimate reality, of a duality based on good and evil, god and the devil. The danger lies in 'neutrality' or what I have previously called 'passivity' or 'inertia', for the duality of existence can only be truly seen when man is positive. He must be totally violent, totally sexual, totally gluttonous. The novel is called an 'eschatological spy novel' because it deals in the flesh (and hence the spirit) through gross eating, carnal lusts, and horrifying murder. Unfortunately the novel contains too many elements, too many characters symbolizing separate strands of the theory, so that one cannot help but be confused. Yet the story can be read purely as a James Bond type thriller. It has a totally involved hero, Dennis Hillier, it has Goldfinger type manipulators, such as Theodorescu and his beautiful accomplice Miss Devi. It has spy and counter spy, plot and twist and counter plot. It even has sex, violence and lots of action.

The trouble is that the novel changes its tracks half way through. It begins with the tale of Roper, Hillier's boyhood friend, who defected to the Russians, because he lost his faith in Catholicism and then in patriotism. He tried to renew both these convictions first through Brigitte his German (and also Nazi) wife, who lets him down by turning prostitute; and then through communism, which also lets him down in the end. But the novel soon proves to have little more than a functional narrative interest in Roper, and follows Hillier instead. In Hillier, Burgess has found a character very similar to Mailer's Stephen Rojack in *An American Dream*. Indeed, Burgess shares with Norman Mailer a hatred of totalitarianism, a fear that this is where today's passivity will lead, and a belief in the romantic nature of violence, on the grounds that it is symbolic of commitment and assertion.

Hillier needs to act. He rapes Brigitte after he has discovered her prostitution. He also takes Clara, a young girl
who is more like a daughter to him. Embarking on a
gastronomic cruise, he is drawn into an orgy of overeating
with Theodorescu, the description of which is likely to send
any reader to the rails, and he also enters an orgy of murders
at the end of the novel, as plot and counterplot unfold
before our bewildered eyes. Murder becomes, not the
ultimate evil, but the ultimate dialogue of reality—it is
interesting to see that again there is a parallel treatment in
Norman Mailer's writings.

Hillier's eyes were drawn to the weapon; if he were to engage in the
ultimate intimacy, he had at least to know its name. It was a Pollock 45,
beautifully looked after.

Any description of the narrative is bound to confuse, as too
much happens to too many disparate characters. The novel
begins on a realistic level with Roper and Hillier at school
together, facing the problems of Catholic dogma, as it
presents itself to bright youthful minds. The development
of Hillier's spying on Roper marks a neat twist in their
friendship. But, as the novel continues, the characters
become 'enciphered' and it is the reader who is then involved in decoding the hidden messages.

It is not until the last few pages, when we discover that
Hillier the spy has become Hillier the priest, that the novel's
philosophical meaning is made apparent. Hillier the spy-
priest says:

'We're too insignificant to be attacked by either the forces of light
or the forces of darkness. And yet, playing the game, we occasionally
let evil in. Evil tumbles in, unaware. But there is no good to fight the
evil with. That's when one grows sick of the game and wants to resign
from it.'

Hillier, an Irish priest, directs the reader into the knowledge that the whole grotesque story has been a discussion,
in quasi-theological terms, based on Manichaeism. This
religion, which originated in the third century AD and com-
bined Gnostic, Christian and Pagan elements was based on a

dualistic theology of light and darkness, good and evil, God
and Satan, the soul and the body: it envisages a perpetual
conflict between the demons and the angels, for the possession
of mankind. Hillier reveals that everything is a great imposture
of the real war that goes on in heaven. Just as East and West
fight it out in our world, with spies intermingling for
possession of the 'body politic', so is the great heavenly war
taking place with priests as the subversive elements.

It is the duality that keeps life going, the tension of the
opposites. This is a difficult thesis, but relates again to
Burgess's despair at 'spiritual death', because it is neutrality
and inertia that stultify this tension or duality. He sees that
what we need are '. . . new terms. God and Notgod.
Salvation and damnation of equal dignity, the two sides of
the coin of ultimate reality.' It is as if he is saying he has lost
his religion that was a part of his upbringing, and what *he*
needs, too, is a renewed faith in something.

This renewal of religious fervour, or of vitality in life is
also dramatized in *The Wanting Seed*, along with a discussion
of his metaphysical theories, followed through several
generations of a nation's life. In a way, it is again an expression of Burgess's intellectual despair, for his vision is of a
cyclic pattern of history that takes nations from socialism to
authoritarianism and back again. *The Wanting Seed* is a
picaresque tale of the adventures of Tristram and Beatrice
Foxe, in this land in the future. The story moves between
different locations and different times. Its form necessarily
leads to an episodic structure that does not hang very closely
together.

In fact, *The Wanting Seed's* significance is to be found as
much in its ideas as in its imagination and its black humour.
The philosophical theory of the novel is put into the mouth of
Tristram in the guise of a history teacher. He teaches that
history follows three phases. First, the Pelagian phase or
'Pelphase' (named after a British monk who believed in
human perfectibility), a theory which Burgess repeats in
Urgent Copy in an essay on Graham Greene. In this era, the

forces of liberal humanism are at work. Everyone expects the best, people believe in man's innate goodness. Over-population is treated by contraception and/or homosexuality; reformation subsumes punishment. There is no discipline. This is followed by the Interphase of transition and then we go into the Augustinian phase or 'Gusphase' which is one of strict discipline, with the stress on human depravity. Discipline and punishment return along with hetero-sexuality and fertility. Wars are organized and arranged for keeping the population down ('extermination sessions'). Then the more liberal attitudes creep back and the cycle begins again.

The narrative contains some of Burgess's most imagina-tive work. It involves a vision of an England in the future (owing something to both Huxley and Orwell of course), and an England whose urban sprawl has enveloped London, Lowestoft, Brighton and Birmingham. In the Pelphase, childbirth is frowned upon and homosexuality is condoned. Beatrice Foxe, Tristram's wife, becomes pregnant by her brother-in-law, Derek, who has been pretending homo-sexual status in order to get on in their world. Beatrice runs away to the North, which is relatively uncivilized, to a State Farm where her sister Mavis is married to the natural, unaffected Shonny and where children and nature are not frowned upon. The tale becomes truly horrific with the account of her struggle to have the baby and of Tristram's macabre adventures. He is thrown into prison, only released as the Gusphase takes over from the Pelphase. As the new order takes over, the people who are starved of food and humanity, suddenly find new life and sexuality: 'The crop had failed and a faithful sow was dying but a new life was preparing to thumb its nose at the forces of sterility.' The novel ends with Tristram wandering the country, where he discovers with amazement a pagan renewal of life which involves cannibalism, and acceptance of the flesh and the spirit. It is a sort of neo-Catholicism in which human flesh is consecrated instead of the host.

IV.   THE LANGUAGE

On the narrative level, then, Burgess's novels may be said
to be based on societies in transition: within the resulting
social flux Burgess perceives much that forms the basis of
human nature and its failures. On the intellectual level, they
are novels concerned with the author's own transition from
a Catholic upbringing to some new belief. But novels are
an art form based not only on social and intellectual per-
ceptions, but also on words, and Burgess is one of the few
authors writing today in England who makes the fullest use
of the raw materials of writing, that is the words themselves.
His linguistic explorations or experiments make him at
once one of our most adventurous writers; they also make
him a difficult writer, for the experiments are often esoteric,
academic, and cut him off, to a certain extent, from the
ordinary reader. One has always to remember that Burgess
is not only a skilful craftsman in the construction of plots
and his creation of characters, but also an extremely clever
and agile-minded man, who draws upon all the resources
of knowledge in his writing. Some of his novels could
perhaps benefit by a glossary.

At least a third of his total output is critical work. This
fact should not be forgotten in a study of his fiction, if only
for the clues which it provides to his fictional imagination
and the theories behind the writing. From such works as
*Here Comes Everybody: An Introduction to James Joyce for
the ordinary reader* (1965) and *The Novel Now* (1967) we
learn about his artistic theories and views on creativity.
As a writer he feels that words are his trade. He sees himself
as a professional, who on the one hand has to come to terms
with publishers' deadlines and the need to earn a living, and
who on the other hand, has not only his readers to serve but
also the world of literature. An accomplished musician as
well as writer, he finds that his approach to the written word
is more aural than visual, and the only writers for whom he

admits any respect, are those similarly inspired: such as Shakespeare, Joyce and Nabokov.

Burgess has suffered to an unjustified degree from critics who have mocked him for his 'productivity', and there are times when his treatises on the novel are barbed with his own self-defence. In *The Novel Now* he justifies his own part in helping to overpopulate the world of books by explaining that as an author he has half-invented people and half-conceived actions that need completion and release. He says he is not romantic in his view of art, but rather cold-bloodedly professional. If the critics and commentators find anything of any worth in what he writes, then obviously he is pleased. But he himself can see only good in fecundity, because of his need to earn and his fears of untimely death.

The serious threat of a suspected brain tumour, which first prompted him to the massive output of five novels in one year, seems to have left him with a desire to cheat death. And there are times when his energy, both physical and imaginative, is overpowering. As one critic of his survey of contemporary literature, *The Novel Now*, deduced from its bibliography, it seemed as if Burgess had been reading one contemporary novel a day, Sundays off, for the then six years of his active writing career. His general reading and his general and specific knowledge cannot pass unappraised.

His theories of the writer of course find expression in his novels too; especially in the Enderby diptych, and in the fictional creation of Shakespeare's life *Nothing like the Sun* (1964). *Inside Mr Enderby* was first published in 1963 under the pseudonym Joseph Kell as part of a longer novel. Burgess was then under sentence of a year to live and he rushed the first part to the publishers, only finishing the greater work in 1968, published as *Enderby Outside*. Enderby is one of Burgess's most sympathetic characters. He is a minor poet who voluntarily withdraws from a world of sharks, fools, exploiters and shady little people. Enderby would rather be involved in no action and with no people.

Yet he is dragged into more than his fair share.

Enderby is one of the best examples of Burgess's type of humour. The comic satire of the novels is based on Enderby himself who is part mocked and part respected. In *Inside Mr Enderby*, the basic image is of the poet retiring to his lavatory to write poetry, the bathtub full of bits of paper. The novel is not crammed with extra characters. Enderby meets Vesta Bainbridge, a glamorous widow from the pop world and employee of 'Fem' girls' magazine, who persuades him into marriage. He is alarmed by the expected level of sexuality and intimacy of the relationship, and eventually escapes. The other major character is Rawcliffe, a decadent and deceitful poet, who has achieved a little more worldly success through expediency. Rawcliffe significantly steals one of Enderby's ideas and makes money and fame out of turning it into a film. Depressed by the disappearance of his Muse after these adventures, Enderby attempts suicide, is discovered, cured and delivered to Wapenshaw, a behavioural psychiatrist who robs him of his poetic gift and makes him 'normal'. Enderby becomes Hogg, a bartender, and we leave him thus disguised.

Enderby Outside begins with Enderby-Hogg just beginning to relocate his poetic gift. He visits Wapenshaw to tell him the good news, but in an admirable satire of modern psychiatric methods, the doctor is furious, as Hogg had taken pride of place in a new book of case histories. The reversal quite destroys the case. Enderby's adventures become more picaresque now. Vesta has married again, into the pop world, to singer Yod Crewsey who is achieving much fame and idolatry as a poet (an episode suggested by Beatle John Lennon's ventures into poetry?). Enderby recognizes the poems as his own, stolen by Vesta, and through no fault of his own becomes accused of Crewsey's murder. He escapes the country—the theme of the traveller without suitcase is popular with Burgess, witness *The Doctor is Sick*, and *The Right to an Answer*, where both Spindrift and Denham find themselves in such a dilemma, and it may be that the fear of being unidentifiable as a traveller is symptomatic of the modern confusion, chaos and nightmare—but again he falls prey to Woman, this time a selenographer, Miranda Boland. He arrives in Tangier, where he meets a group of weird poets spawned by the psychedelic revolution (his own friend the writer William Burroughs lives in Tangier). He again encounters Rawcliffe, who reminds him of his mortality, and finally what seems to be the representative of his own Muse, a strange young girl who has a thing or two to tell him about his art: 'Poetry isn't a silly little hobby to be practised in the smallest room of the house.'

In these two novels, there are several different types of people in the service of art. There are pop singers and drug addicts who, to the accomplished musician and literarily educated Burgess, mock both music and words; and the various women Vesta, Miranda, and the girl/Muse who all try to reawaken Enderby, through sex, to his artistic failings. But failure or not, Enderby is at least the one who retains his integrity. He may be funny, he may be pathetic, but he is still their superior. His type of poetry is traditional, and craftsmanlike. He is perhaps the equivalent to Burgess the novelist, not writing out of any great commitment to Art and the Muse, but writing because he feels a love of words and the need to write.

Perhaps poetry is part of Burgess's general view of the cosmic joke and the irony of life, namely that those who feel the inspiration to write are not necessarily going to be great. But at least they achieve more than those who exploit art. As a traditionalist himself, who has said that he sees himself not quite in the pot-boiler category, but not in the *avant-garde* either ('Letter from England', *Hudson Review*, Autumn 1966), he identifies with Enderby, whose Muse figure admonishes him: 'You lack courage. You've been softened by somebody or something. You're frightened of the young and the experimental and the way-out and the black dog.'

Enderby, like Edwin Spindrift the linguist, as we have seen earlier, is happiest in the world of words, unrelated to life. Out of this idea comes one very important theme: the conflict within Burgess himself about the nature of creativity. A linguist, and a musician who says he approaches writing through aural images, Burgess obviously finds the idea of the ivory towers of academe a pleasant ground for the sensitive artist, for whom society and involvement are too much. Burgess himself found that he had to live in exile, and has often been quoted in interviews as expressing his dislike of life, in the sense that its only interest to him is in his being able to withdraw from it and to produce these bizarre characters from his imagination or observation. Yet this dream of a hermit-like existence conflicts with his predominant feeling that creativity comes from the expenditure of energy, and that entails total involvement. The embodiment of creativity and energy is Shakespeare, whom he characterized in *Nothing like the Sun*, but before we discuss that novel, there are certain statements in Burgess's first novel, *A Vision of Battlements*, that lend some light to these ideas.

In his last essay in *Urgent Copy*, Burgess has recorded that he first felt inspired to write when he arrived in Gibraltar: where he sensed the past both of European civilizations and of a Catholic environment. Richard Ennis, a failed musician waiting in Gibraltar for the chance to return to England now the war is over, suffers the same kind of sexual alienation experienced by Enderby, Crabbe, Howarth and Denham. He wants to compose music, but lacks the energy or the drive. He meets Lavinia in Gibraltar, a sort of goddess who writes poetry. But he finds her manner forceful and not inspiring, and he wishes 'he were back in the billet with Julian, in the calm epicene atmosphere, where lust could be transmuted into creative energy'. Ennis has been sharing a billet with Julian, a homosexual. There is no strong implication that he is homosexual himself, just that he enjoys the calm, cool, unimpassioned atmosphere in which he feels he would be able to write (or compose).

In the same novel, Lavinia quotes these lines from a Shakespeare sonnet:

> The expense of spirit in a waste of shame
> Is lust in action, and till action, lust
> Is perjured, murderous, bloody, full of blame.

which neatly sums up Burgess's conflict; a desire for the epicene coolness of non-involvement (with more than a hint of homosexuality), contrasted with the belief that in order for creative energy to be released, one has to give way to all one's lusts and be totally involved in life. Of the title *Nothing like the Sun*, Burgess has said, it emphasizes the impossibility for us of conveying the authentic effulgence (the Sun).

WS (Burgess's fictional Shakespeare) may not have been able to emulate the energy of the sun, but he certainly threw himself into life, finding himself the mere plaything of the gods' will. His lusts took him away from those he really loved, destroyed all his better purposes, and eventually his own health. Behind this tale of WS's adventures we hear Ted Arden's (from *The Right to an Answer*) voice moralizing on his ancestor's ways: 'Will really is a terrible example for everybody, showing what happens when you leave the wife of your bosom and go off whoring after other women. . . .' The cruelty of life's irony is perceived by no one more piquantly than WS. In London, away from his family, he receives the message that his son Hamnet is dying: WS grinned wearily, 'We are all caught, are we not, between two worlds? Our sin and our sickness is not to choose one and turn our backs on the other, but to hanker after both!' And in Lear-like despair he dreams of what he might have hankered after given another life, through his vision of the life Hamnet might have had. For him he desires, not this lusting after the flesh, and writing plays by the dozen, but a life of sterility; that intellectual world of literature and learning mentioned by Richard Ennis.

In these thoughts Burgess makes WS admit to a confusion in his ideas. He thinks of Hamnet, 'he could not act, but he had no need to act: no violent assumption of commitment could ever come to disturb his sad calm'. Burgess's WS dreams secretly of that stoic calm, yet knows that literature comes from that other way of life; that the force of literature is no more nor less than a copy of the force of life.

Let us have no nonsensical talk about merging and melting souls, though binary suns, two spheres in a single orbit. There is the flesh and the flesh makes all. Literature is an epiphenomenon of the action of the flesh.

Next to God, Burgess has said, Shakespeare created most. *Nothing like the Sun* was, according to the author, his tribute to the great master for the quatercentenary year (1964). It was also, it seems obvious, an opportunity for Burgess to match his skills against Shakespeare's. In filling in the blanks about his life, he was able to furnish the character of WS with his own image, but, above all, he was able to emulate Shakespeare's mastery of the language. So, young WS is seen talking, thinking, and day-dreaming in language that leads on to his playwriting without any real break. In such a passage as follows, is an example of Burgess's thorough understanding of Shakespeare's words and imagery:

Goat. Willow. Widow. Tarquin, superb sun-black southern king, all awry, twisted snakewise, had goatlike gone to it. So *tragos*, a tragedy. Razor and whetstone, But that was the other Tarquin. . . . But a willow was right for death.

The language of the whole novel is a remarkable achievement of taut, packed sentences, Elizabethan phraseology and again as in *A Clockwork Orange*, the invention of a new vernacular to fit the society in question. Shakespeare has remained a preoccupation with Burgess over the years and he has since completed a more factual account of his life and works in the large illustrated volume entitled *Shakespeare* (1970). He is also reputedly working on a film script for a Hollywood musical of Shakespeare. Shakespeare is Burgess's type of writer. He wrote, it could be maintained, not out of any great love for art, but for money and status in this life. He wanted to become a gentleman. He was also a writer very much aware of the musical qualities of language and very much in love with the sound of words. But Shakespeare's love for words is superseded for Burgess by James Joyce, to whom he has devoted a lot of time and energy in the preparation of *Here Comes Everybody* (1965) and *A Shorter Finnegans Wake* (1968) (in which he has cut the text down for the more bewildered reader).

Joyce is, to Burgess, the supreme example of the proper difference between literature and the popular novel. Joyce uses his knowledge of languages (both he and Burgess mastered at least six or seven), and his knowledge of literature throughout his writing. Burgess's admiration for Joyce's work is important to notice with regard to Burgess's most recent book *MF*, in which Burgess employs all his knowledge of linguistics, literary and mythical allusions, even fashionable intellectual theories. Reading his essay and reviews in *Urgent Copy* can again help. For there, Burgess explains the source of the Algonquin legend upon which he has based the novel *MF*. It is a tale he derived from an essay by Claude Lévi-Strauss, 'The Scope of Anthropology', which deals with Lévi-Strauss's views on myths and riddles. It is a complicated story of Oedipus-like origins that involves incest which Burgess relates to that other family— of languages.

The narrative in *MF* is an odd mixture of grotesque nightmare and fairy tale. It is not particularly successful as a novel of conventional standards; it is more a work of, shall we say, comprehensive literariness which Burgess has always admired and understood, in Joyce. The guiding idea is that literature, as language, should work in areas of total experience; that analysis is contemporary and sophisticated practice. In *Language Made Plain*, Burgess's book on linguistics, he explains that primitive people did not speak in pidgin English, rather they spoke in synthetic terms, that understood a total experience. Joyce writes in the same way, in what we refer to as 'epiphanies' or moments of revelation. And Burgess has attempted that style here.

MF is an erudite, sophisticated novel, that could benefit from a glossary, though Burgess would be the first to refute this. Unfortunately, if the ordinary reader's knowledge is not on a par with the author's, this resetting of the ancient myth of the Iroquois Indians may not have any special appeal. However, when *Finnegans Wake* was criticized for being too erudite and beyond the normal reader, Burgess defended it by saying we must become as erudite as Joyce. In criticizing the wealth of Joyce's mind, he felt reviewers were saying that his great crime was to know too much. Indeed, how can it be a crime to write a truly literary novel, fulfilling, as Burgess describes it in *Here Comes Everybody*, 'the author's egotistical desire not merely to add to English Literature but to enclose what is already there'. Yet in concentrating on the erudite, on the literary, Burgess may be letting down his ordinary reader, in *MF*, no longer making those witty and comic comments on our society which make his great body of writing such a gift to contemporary English literature.

ANTHONY BURGESS

A Select Bibliography

(Place of publication, London unless stated otherwise)

Separate Works:

TIME FOR A TIGER (1956). *Novel*

THE ENEMY IN THE BLANKET (1958). *Novel*

ENGLISH LITERATURE: A SURVEY FOR STUDENTS (1958). *Criticism*

BEDS IN THE EAST (1959). *Novel*

THE RIGHT TO AN ANSWER (1960). *Novel*
—revised 1970.

THE DOCTOR IS SICK (1960). *Novel*

DEVIL OF A STATE (1961). *Novel*

ONE HAND CLAPPING (1961). *Novel*
—published under the pseudonym Joseph Kell.

THE WORM AND THE RING (1961). *Novel*

THE WANTING SEED (1962). *Novel*

A CLOCKWORK ORANGE (1962). *Novel*

HONEY FOR THE BEARS (1963). *Novel*

INSIDE MR ENDERBY (1963). *Novel*
—first published under the pseudonym Joseph Kell and reissued, 1966, under his own name.

THE NOVEL TODAY (1963). *Criticism*

NOTHING LIKE THE SUN (1964). *Fictional biography*

THE EVE OF ST VENUS (1964). *Novel*

LANGUAGE MADE PLAIN (1964). *Linguistics*

HERE COMES EVERYBODY (1965). *Criticism*

A VISION OF BATTLEMENTS (1965). *Novel*

TREMOR OF INTENT (1966). *Novel*

THE NOVEL NOW (1967). *Criticism*

URGENT COPY (1968). *Critical Essays*

A SHORTER FINNEGANS WAKE (1968)
—a shortened version of Joyce's novel.

ENDERBY OUTSIDE (1968). *Novel*

SHAKESPEARE (1970). *Criticism*

MF (1971). *Novel*

Critical Studies:

THE GOD I WANT, ed. J. Mitchell (1967).

'Mr Enderby and Mr Burgess', by G. Aggeler, *Malahat Review*, X, April 1969.

'The Comic Art of Anthony Burgess', by G. Aggeler, *Arizona Quarterly*, XXV, Autumn 1969.

THE SITUATION OF THE NOVEL, by B. Bergonzi (1970).

'Recent British Fiction: Some Established Writers', by F. McDowell, *Contemporary Literature*, Summer 1970.

'Death Without Tears: Anthony Burgess's dissolution of the West', by W. Sullivan, *Hollins Critic*, VI, ii.

WRITERS AND THEIR WORK